CRISIS

No matter what the crisis is, you can rule in the midst.

Wilma Foster

CRISIS

Unless otherwise indicated, all scripture quotations are taken from the King James Version (KJV) of the Holy Bible.

Cover Design: Alexandria Stubblefield

Published by Anyanwu Productions
In Partnership with the
Daughters of Deborah Ministries, Inc.
Wichita, Kansas 67226

ISBN: 978-1-930183-11-7 (digital)
ISBN: 978-1-930183-12-4 (paperback)

DEDICATION

In memory of my first born, granddaughter/daughter ~ Gabriella Loree Curry ~ my motivation to not give up and who was so infamously given my mother's first name as her middle name as a namesake.

TABLE OF CONTENTS

ACKNOWLEDGMENT

I thank God. I acknowledge first my Lord and Savior, Jesus Christ. From Him, all blessings flow, resulting in me even attempting and completing such a project. It was Him who put in my heart and spirit this work to contribute to humanity. I thank Him for even considering me as being valuable enough to give it to others, a means whereby they can reach up and hold on to His hands more tightly, more firmly, and to be able to walk out these words on paper. I am grateful to serve as my Brother's Keeper and hold on to its readers' hand as they travel through the dark places of life. So, I thank Him for the opportunity to give.

I thank my husband, Apostle Henry A. Foster, for loving me through all I have attempted to do and advancing the Kingdom of God on earth. I also thank God for my Breakthrough Ministries family, which consists of spiritual and natural children together as one. I thank Him for how they consistently pray for me and the visions that God has given me to be able to birth these visions, and they become more than just images on canvas, but the living will of God on the earth.

INTRODUCTION

To every thing there is a season, and a time to every purpose under the heaven: Ecclesiastes 3:1

How many of you have heard the word crisis? What definition comes to mind when you think of the word crisis? You don't have to because I have written it down here for you. A crisis is defined as a time of intense, not just difficulty, but intense difficulty, which means it's a more of an extreme situation. Of course, we all know what having challenging times means. We experienced them, but the definition of crisis is a time of intense, magnified difficulty...trouble magnified trouble. Such times tend to be a season that people are not happy about or are not full of joy when such times come.

***

Have you ever had trouble that was not just a problem but also a magnified one? A time of trouble could be as simple as experiencing some difficulty with one person at your job or school. Magnified trouble could be you have been falsely accused of something and lost your job at a time when you have just been diagnosed with a medical condition. Or what about experiencing danger? Perhaps you've been in a situation where if you're like me, you had a gun pulled on you, and the person told you that they were about to blow your brains out. That's a crisis, and all you can remember is what your mother told you, and that is, when you don't know what to do, call on the name of Jesus. You couldn't talk the potential shooter down because he was ready to kill himself. Kill you first and then himself.

Regardless of the length or details of the crisis, we can come through it. We can still grow in the midst of them. We can come out of them victorious and stronger than before the crisis. This can only be accomplished with a total dependency on the Lord God Almighty. Many of us don't look like what we have been through. I don't look like what I've been through. There is a song, *I Don't Look Like (What I've Been Through)* by Deon Kipping, which speaks to experiencing a crisis and seeing ourselves on the other side of it. Every time I hear it, I get teary. It is because the Lord God has brought me and others through every crisis victoriously. Despite the situation and what we went through, our life right now doesn't look like what we've been through.

***

The purpose of this book is to encourage and help its readers to learn what God is asking and expecting us to do in the midst of a crisis. Readers are reminded that while a crisis is intense and uncomfortable, it has an expiration date. Not only does it have an expiration date, but it is also possible to move through it without being overtaken by fear. Rather, our decision and position can be one of ruling and reigning in the midst of a crisis **UNTIL**. And that **UNTIL** is the moment that we possess the victorious breakthrough, deliverance, and the end to the crisis.

Throughout the book, direct quotes are indicated using italicized words or sections. Additionally, there are scriptures to help you learn what God's Word says about crisis and how to navigate it. It is recommended to use the scriptures to encourage yourself and exercise your faith by choosing to believe, standing on, and confessing what God has said in His Word.

> Joshua 1:8 *This book of the law shall not depart out of thy mouth; but thou shalt meditate therein day and night, that thou mayest observe to do according to all that is written therein: for then thou shalt make thy way prosperous, and then thou shalt have good success.*

> Psalm 1:2 *But his delight is in the law of the Lord; and in his law doth he meditate day and night.*

It is also recommended that you lean on and trust in the person of the Holy Spirit to reveal to you and expand your understanding about and comprehend what the Lord Jesus Christ is saying to us concerning our crisis. So, that you can walk through your crisis, expecting to see your promised victory manifest, and then obtain it.

1 THE CRISIS

⁸ We are troubled on every side, yet not distressed; we are perplexed, but not in despair; ⁹ Persecuted, but not forsaken; cast down, but not destroyed; 2 Corinthians 4:8-9

Throughout my life, I have experienced a number of different difficulties. Some were the result of bad decisions. The bad decisions would include connecting with the wrong people and engaging in activities that didn't align with what I had been taught. Others were the result of choosing to follow after God and the enemy coming after me. We, as believers, know that following Christ doesn't mean our lives will be all roses and no thorns or that we will have no trouble. In fact, it means the complete opposite. We know this because God's Word let's us know what we can expect in this life.

Memory Scriptures:

> Psalm 34: 19 - *Many are the afflictions of the righteous: but the Lord delivereth him out of them all.*

John 10:10 - *The thief cometh not, but for to steal, and to kill, and to destroy: I am come that they might have life, and that they might have it more abundantly.*

John 16:33 - *These things I have spoken unto you, that in me ye might have peace. In the world ye shall have tribulation: but be of good cheer; I have overcome the world.*

1 Corinthians 10:13 - *There hath no temptation taken you but such as is common to man: but God is faithful, who will not suffer you to be tempted above that ye are able; but will with the temptation also make a way to escape, that ye may be able to bear it.*

Regardless of the reasons or the details of the crisis, a crisis is a tough place. Such seasons consist of varying experiences that come together to form intense trouble.

***

Today, people all over the world have or are experiencing crises. In the Scriptures, our examples included Moses, Ruth, David, Jesus, the Apostles, and the early Church. It is not uncommon for people to be faced with intense difficulty. The details of their crisis can involve or affect several aspects of life, such as their health. Some news may be coming down the pipe that might shake some people. Others may experience intense difficulty in their marriage and/or relationships. At the same time, others may be faced with the death or separation of those who hold a dear place in their hearts. Each experience can weigh on us differently and affect us mentally, emotionally, and physically.

This thing called crisis is very real. Many people find themselves in a place of crisis. A critical thing to do is to keep your mind on Jesus. If you don't, you'll risk being pulled under the crisis. What comes to mind here is swimming. When swimmers find themselves in a place of a rip current or undertow, they can be at risk of being pulled under the water. I don't want that. I am also sure that you don't want that either. I've heard of people being pulled under, being unable to break free, and they drown. This can happen because people become overwhelmed, fearful, anxious, panicking, and/or disoriented. When this happens, even a skilled swimmer can be pulled under the water or under the pressure of a crisis. Again, I don't want to do that. I don't want that to happen to you either. To prevent this, we must learn how to navigate our seasons of crisis.

***

My last crisis occurred in 2024. I had no idea that the year would go as it did. The season would begin with the Lord revealing the hearts of those who walked closely with me in ministry. The season grew to include challenges closer to home and my heart, including the death of my oldest granddaughter and brother. While I did not fret or consider their deaths as a loss because I knew they died having known Christ, both deaths were unexpected. The season also included a continuation or revisiting of prior challenges. Overall, in that season, I faced multiple experiences that contributed to my season of crisis, which could be summarized as a season of intense difficulty, a time of revelation, loss, disappointment, and grief. Throughout this crisis, I experienced stress, heartache, pain, and disappointment and struggled with understanding some things until the Lord gave me clarity about them. Learning to navigate the crisis was critical. Trusting God through it all was even more vital. And expecting to see His promises (e.g., of help, victory, peace) was mandatory.

***

What crises are you facing today? You may be experiencing what has been already mentioned or some other form of intense difficulty. You may be faced with a single crisis or a complex or long-season crisis consisting of multiple crises.

Take a few moments and write down details about your crisis. Is it one or more crises or things going on contributing to your season of crisis? How long have you been in this season? It may take a few times of reflection. Ask the Holy Spirit to help you identify your crises or the source(s) of this intense difficulty. Also, write down your feelings and thoughts you had/are having during this crisis.

_____

_____

_____

_____

_____

_____

_____

_____

_____

_____

_____

_____

_____

_____

_____

_____

_____

_____

_____

_____

_____

_____

_____

_____

_____

_____

Know that just because we're going through a crisis, it doesn't mean that God gives up on His expectations for us. So, what is it that He expects of us? Although we're in these strong, turbulent times filled with crises, we must choose to remember, be who we are, and do what He expects. Father God expects us to act like we know who we are. Do you know who you are? This may sound like a silly question to ask believers. However, unfortunately, some believers allow the world, or worldly systems, to define who they are and govern what they can and cannot do. This dependency on worldly standards and ungodly ideas can lead to a loss of identity, confusion, and stagnation. It is important that we see and define ourselves by what He says. Otherwise, we put undue burdens and limits on God and ourselves.

***

So, who are you? Who does God say that we are? **Take a few moments** and using either a concordance, the reference/index in the back of your Bible, and/or an online reliable search tool (e.g., secure bible app), **locate three scriptures that highlight what God says you are or how He sees you.**

_____

_____

_____

_____

_____

_____

_____

_____

_____

_____

_____

_____

_____

_____

_____

_____

_____

_____

_____

_____

_____

_____

_____

We must see ourselves like our Heavenly Father sees us. To Him, we are the children of God (Romans 8:16). For those who have accepted Christ's sacrifice on behalf of their sins, God lives on the inside of us (John 3:16; 1 Timothy 2:5; 1 John 4:4). Greater is He that is in us. So, even though you are going through it, God still has expectations for you. He never stops expecting greatness from you, no matter how it feels. Let me remind you that He can expect greatness because He knows what you have inside, starting with the Greater One who lives inside you and me.

Today, you and I are going to go through crises in life. However, as saints of God, we must learn and depend on God's Word for guidance regarding navigating this season. We should use His Word as a reminder for ourselves. His Word should also be used to help with guidance regarding what to pray so that God will prepare you for whatever is coming at you as part of your season of crisis. Otherwise, what else are you going to do? Are you going to turn your back on the Lord? Are you going to doubt that God is moving? Or what are you going to do? Are you going to man up, woman up, and say, come on, Lord, let's go. If your answer is yes, then let's see what He is expecting us to do in the midst of the crisis.

2 IN THE MIDST

For God hath not given us the spirit of fear; but of power, and of love, and of a sound mind. 2 Timothy 1:7

In the midst of the crisis, God does not want us to be afraid. So, we're not to be fearful. Know that we don't need to run. We don't need to tuck our tails. We don't need to get in a corner and say, I'm going to stay here **until** the Lord returns and takes me home as part of the Rapture. No, this is not what he's saying? Since this is not what He is saying, let's see then what He is saying in the Word of God. First let's visit Psalms 110:1-2:

> *[1] The Lord said unto my Lord, sit thou at my right hand, until I make thine enemies thy footstool. [2] The Lord shall send the rod of thy strength out of Zion: rule thou in the midst of thine enemies.*

In the first one, we read that *the Lord said unto my Lord, Sit thou at my until.* Now, He said, ***Until.*** Remember that word, ***until***. Until I make what? Verse two says, *the LORD shall send what the rod of thy strength out of Zion.* Wait a minute. Do you see what I am seeing? *Rule thou in the midst of thine enemies?* You may question whether you read that correctly, but I assure you, you did. Yes, there's an ***until*** rule...***until*** I make your enemies be a footstool. So, in the midst of your crisis, rule in the midst of your enemies. This is not a mere suggestion, but a certain promise from the Lord.

***

I don't know about your current crisis, but I will tell you one thing you need to know: it is seasonal. What did I say about crises being seasonal? Every crisis in our life is seasonal. In the winter season, the length of the season may be prolonged. You may even grow tired of it and long for a different season. Regardless of how long it appears, it doesn't last forever. It doesn't last throughout the year or every year thereafter without ending. It has its designated allotment of time. And so, it is a crisis in our lives. Let's revisit verse one and re-read it until it becomes Rhema to you. Psalms 110:1:

> [1] *The Lord said unto my Lord, sit thou at my right hand,* ***until*** *I make thine enemies thy footstool.*

There is one word that you need to grasp, and that is ***until***. The ***until*** is a place of waiting, a period of hopeful anticipation. Did you hear me? Yes, the ***until*** means that you'll have to *let patience do her perfect work* (James 1:4). You will have to know that God is an on-time God and that He has not forgotten about you. ***Until...***, He says, *Sit thou at my right hand.* So, be patient, for all will be revealed in His time.

Let's move back to the beginning of the verse and first take notice of it saying that the *Lord said unto my Lord.* Do you know who's talking here? This is God prophetically speaking about the Messiah. He's talking about the position of the Lord Jesus Christ. In this verse, God is talking about the placement of rulership with Him. He says to His Son:

> *Many crises are going to come your way, Messiah, but I want you to know that you're going to rule. And every problem you encounter and every trick of the enemy that's going to come to try to cause you to abort My plan and will for you on the earth, will not prosper. I will make your enemies your footstool. So, rule and reign* **until**.

God then speaks to us, saying to us to rule and reign. You may wonder how we can rule and reign. Here, as believers, we need to remember what God's Word says about us and our given authority in Christ Jesus to rule and reign. We know that in accepting Jesus and entering the Kingdom of God, we gained power and authority (Matthew 28:18; Luke 10:19). Furthermore, just as Jesus is seated at the right hand of the Father (Mark 16:19; Hebrews 1:3), we too are seated at the right hand of God in Christ Jesus.

***

To bring clarity to us being seated at the right hand of the Father, let's go to Ephesians 2:6:

> *⁶And hath raised us up together, and made us sit*

together in heavenly places in Christ Jesus

In Ephesians 2:6, the Apostle Paul informs believers that we have been raised together. He goes on to write that we, believers, the saints of God, are also sitting together in Christ Jesus. So, the Apostle Paul says God has raised us and made us sit together with Christ. And where is He seated? He is seated at the right hand of Father God. This signifies our authority in Christ. We, as believers, have a position of ruling, empowered by our shared authority with Christ. Just as Father was speaking to our Lord about making His enemies His footstool, know that Father God is also talking to us. He told us: *There's a **until** because I'm going to make every enemy your footstool.* We can't help but ask how God will do it?

While people often use the word footstool, I don't know if we understand it. The footstool simply means **until** He eradicates this. **Until** He shows you victory. And victory isn't victory **until** it's a manifested victory. He is going to manifest your victory. When Jesus hung on the cross and said, *it is finished* (John 19:30). That translates to V-I-C-T-O-R-Y...victory in Jesus, my Savior forever, victory. After His death at the cross, Jesus our Lord was buried, quickened, resurrected, ascended, and then sat at the right hand of the Father. This victory in Christ should reassure us and fill us with hope, knowing that He has already overcome the world, and we share in His victory.

***

For many of us, God has spoken victory, but we have not seen the manifested victory yet. We have not seen the problem turn into a footstool. We have not gotten to see our intense difficulties and enemies eradicated. Nevertheless, God has promised here that He will give you victory. You're going to get this. Again, I want this to become Rhema to you because you've got to see it. It's one word. I want the light bulb to go off when we read it. *The Lord said unto my Lord, sit thou at my right hand.* Stay with me. Be with me. Eat with me. Cry with me. Tell me about it:

> *Until I know you're going through. Until hardships are all around you. Until the enemy is rushed in what like a flood. Until you didn't ask for this mess. Until nobody's listening to you. Until they don't even care about what you think about the matter. Until, Lord, what am I going to do? Until I don't see where the money is going to come from. Until I'm feeling the pressure because I've never been this way before. Until I don't know how this is going to work out. Until I don't see how the dots are going to connect.*

***

Until God says, *I am going to make your enemy your footstool, but it's only going to come as you remain with Me.* Now, there's also a coward's time coming or already here, but don't give in to it. I encourage you. Don't give up on your **until** moment because, at the appointed time, God will make a way of escape for you. However, He also wants us to rule during our crisis moments. You will have to be like David when you're feeling nervous, or your emotions are all over the place. This is when you will have to command your soul to do what? To be still, say to your soul:

> *Be still my soul. I'm not asking you today. I'm coming in the authority that's been given to me by Jesus, the Son*

of the living God. I will take charge of you today, and so I command you to stop running all over the place. I command you to be still as I wait on God and as I stand firm in the Word of truth that I have heard. Because I'm about to rule on this thing. Come on.

You need to let it be known whose report you believe. Remember yourself and the enemy of your soul that you choose and are ruling now. Let especially the enemy of your soul, the devil, know that:

Yes, I see this crisis, but I believe the report of the Lord. I feel the pain I'm experiencing, the disappointment, and the rejection. I know all of that, but I will not cave in. I will not take it back. Jesus is the Lord of my life. I'm not going to be the dog that returns to his vomit (Proverbs 26:11). He is still God in my life. I will not take it back. I will not change my confession. He reigns in me and my confession, my words that I speak, no matter how you act, no matter what you do, no matter what they say, no matter what they do to me, no matter what they take from me, I stand firm in what God's Word says, which is reign during your time of crisis.

There is also a manifested victory in your and my life. You've got to see Father God eradicate some things. Our responsibility is to stand firm in faith during crisis moments. We're going to. Thus, this is not the time to tuck our tailbones, run and hide. We must choose to stand still and to see. See, what? To see the manifested promise of God because He has promised the *Until.* God is going to get some things out of your way. So, what problem do you have that's so intense that you need God to get rid of it? Tell yourself: *I've got to see the God I serve to eliminate some stuff for me.*

So, you will rule during this crisis period by standing firm in God, standing strong in the Word of God, and standing firm in your faith in God. God says:

> *In your time of crisis, I don't want you to become stagnant. I want you to move. I don't want you to put the dreams I gave you on the shelf until you. Come out of the crisis. I want you to work like there's no crisis at all. I don't want you to shorten your legs. I want you to grow taller in Me. I don't want you to act like your faith is waning. I want you to be like Abraham (Romans 4:1-16). I want you to grow strong in faith. I want you to see who I am in you and through you. You got to square your shoulders back and not cower down during your moment of testing through a crisis, because that's when you're going to see Me.*

Crises come. They're seasonal. They don't last forever. They come, and they go. Those moments come, and they go. You and I cannot get away from a life crisis, but it won't last forever. We will forever be challenged and experience crises, but each crisis has an expiration date. It has to end, but you and I must learn how to endure **until**. You can't get lazy or pity parties. You have to come on and move.

***

Faith is an action word. My husband taught me something. He said, *faith is like a muscle, and you must work it.* If you don't work it, guess what? It's all flabby. You've got to work your faith. Give your faith a job. Assign it to something. Tell your faith:

> *I'm like a tree planted by the waters. I shall not be moved. I am not going anywhere. I'm not losing anything. You are not repossessing my car. You are not taking my house. You are not jacking up my credit. I may have a few slow pays. That's going to fall off after a few years. I serve a God that's able to rewrite my resume. All I have to do is ride the test of time and hang in there.*

Not only do you need to assign your faith a job, but you need to know how to keep your joy and hold on to your peace. These are things the enemy is coming after. The devil is coming to wear out the saints of God. He's coming after our joy and peace. He's coming after we confessed faith. He wants us to change our confession of faith, but come hell or high water, you cannot change your confession. Your confession should be that you believe the Word of God is truth and that God is not a man that He should lie (Numbers 23:19; John 17:17). Remember that God said that He would never leave nor forsake you (1 Kings 8:57; Hebrews 13:5). He said he is always with you. He wants to do me good and not evil (Jeremiah 29:11).

***

Here are to remember in the midst of your crisis:

1 John 4:4 - *Ye are of God, little children, and have overcome them: because* **greater is he that is in you, than he that is in the**

world.

- Remember, you and I can outlast the enemy because we have the Spirit of the Living God down on the inside of us. Father God has already given us everything we need to outlast the enemy's tactics. You can outlast him.

- Remember who you are and Who lives on the inside of you. You have the greater One inside of you. Otherwise, the devil will dupe you and make you think that you're not going to make it through this crisis. Remember that you're coming through this and rule in the midst of your adversity.

Psalms 110:1 - *The Lord said unto my Lord, sit thou at my right hand,* **until** *I make thine enemies thy footstool.*

- Remember to rule in the midst of your crisis. What am I saying? Function in the midst of your crisis and don't cave in. Square your shoulders back.

Hebrews 12:2 - **Looking unto Jesus the author and finisher of our faith;** *who for the joy that was set before him endured the cross, despising the shame, and is set down at the right hand of the throne of God.*

- Continue to live as you go through your crisis, continue to look unto Jesus, who is the Author and the Finisher of our faith, as we go through these seasons.

<u>Notes:</u>

3 AT THE END

Have not I commanded thee? Be strong and of a good courage; be not afraid, neither be thou dismayed: for the Lord, thy God is with thee whithersoever thou goest. Joshua 1:9

At the end of the day, the Lord says, *Fear not*. Isaiah 41, verse ten (Isa. 41:10a) says:

> *"Fear not for thou, for I am with thee, be not dismayed..."* and that dismayed...

Just for clarity's sake, I want you to understand something: the word dismay. Do you know what dismayed was or is? I wrote down several synonyms because I like to know about a word and how to use it effectively. The verse says, *be not dismayed; in* other words, don't feel distressed. Don't allow yourself to be frightened, shaken up, or unsettled; don't get into shock mode. Because why? He...I Am is thy God. Let's read the more of Isaiah 41:10 (starting with Isa 41:10b), God says:

I will strengthen thee, yea, I will help thee, yea, I will uphold thee.

With what? The right hand of His righteousness. Don't get upset when things happen like we see happening in our crisis. He is still your God. He has promised those that are His that He will be with them. So, we all need to daily be real, and say:

Lord, help me. I want you to help me to go through this crisis and bring glory to you. I want to not walk in fear. You said don't be afraid and that You're going to uphold me with Your right hand. I want to keep my trust in you. I don't want to be seeking help from other places. I don't want to be dealing with that old temptation to run here and run there. I want to run to you because you know me. You know all about me. So, I want You to be the One to do what needs to be done in me.

***

Know this: there's a great cloud of witnesses who've come through already (Hebrews 12:1). They've come through the hard places already. They have come through the disappointments. They've come through shame. They have come through it all. Now, they're looking at you. They're looking at me. Why, you ask? They are waiting to see how we are going to manage this adversity. How are you going to manage this crisis?

Remember that crises are a part of life. We can't get away from it. I wish that we could, but do you know what? The crisis is going to have to run its course. I'm tired of experiencing crises. I want to change it. I can identify with you; trust me. I imagine that the Israelites, the children of Israel, got tired of the Midianites coming to steal their goods at the same time, all the time. I know they got tired of that. Sometimes, you and I have to get tired enough to do something about the crisis.

***

Let's go to Hebrews 12:1:

> *Wherefore seeing we also are compassed about with so great a cloud of witnesses, let us lay aside every weight, and the sin which doth so easily beset us, and let us run with patience the race that is set before us,*

Wherefore, seeing we also are compassed about. The Lord dropped this in my spirit, so great a cloud of witnesses. What are they witnessing? What are they saying? Could it be? Could it just be? Let's finish reading Hebrews 12:1 and see if we can get some light on this:

> *...so great a cloud of witnesses, let us lay aside every weight, and the sin which doth so easily beset us, and let us run with patience the race that is set before us,*

These witnesses can attest to what you're going through and what needs to be done. They're witnessing your and my actions and how we live for the Lord. They tell us to hang in there; we've already come through. They're telling us that we, too, can go through.

Today, in the name of the Lord Jesus Christ, *lay aside every weight*, and while you are at it, put off *the sin which doth so easily beset you*. The sin that so easily besets you means there is sin that persistently is a threat to or snare for you. However, let us run with patience after you lay aside the weights and the sin. Don't be quick to give up. Hang in there. Ask God for some staying power. Come on, endurance. Ask God for the spirit of the finisher. I pray that the spirit of the finisher rests upon your shoulders and crowns your head as you go through. There's no stopping, there's no sitting. We have no time for pity parties. Run this race with patience. In Hebrews 12:1, we are instructed and encouraged to do just that. So, let us, the Church of the Lord Jesus Christ, run this race. We're going to give this race a name: crisis. *Let us run with patience*, and it's set before us.

Notice here that there's a comma at the end of verse one of Hebrews chapter twelve. What's the other part? There's no period there. So that tells me it wasn't finished. There's another part to this. Let's take a look at what comes after the comma in verse two (Hebrews 12:2):

> ² *Looking unto Jesus the author and finisher of our faith, who for the joy that was set before him endured the cross, despising the shame, and is set down at the right hand of the throne of God.*

Looking unto Jesus, the Author and Finisher of our faith. Who for the joy? Check it out. Stay focused. *Who for the joy that was set before Him endured.* Endured what? *Endured the cross, despising the shame.* You know that people may be ashamed of you because of the clothes you wear, how you look, or where you live. People may be embarrassed to own us for several reasons, but guess what? It doesn't matter because we have the victory in Christ Jesus.

***

The crisis in our lives is real. Please don't act like you don't have crisis experiences because we all do. However, God says, I want you to reign and rule this time. Could you go through it? Ask God to give you the spirit of the finisher. Ask Him to provide you with some staying power. Cry if you have to, but don't wallow in it. Don't just sit there and go to pieces. You've been this way before. Look at the memorials (the memories of God's goodness) that you have.

How many times has God brought you out of a situation or crisis? I tell you that God has brought me through so many difficulties. I have lost count. We may realize that we have all been through so many battles. Regardless of the number of battles and crises, we must keep before us that if God is before us, who can be against us? Your and my job is to stand upright before God. Our job is to ensure we stand upright before God, but I can't be afraid to go through a crisis. At the end of the day, we must believe and hold on to the promise of the Lord that He will eradicate our enemies and deal with the crisis. The manifested victory will be possessed and not just dreamt about.

***

Notes:

4 THE THIRD DAY

In all things, we must remember that at the end of the day, we live to bring glory to God. It's not about us anyway. We say our life is not our own. Do we mean it, or is it just a cliche?

***

In 2024, I ministered on the word crisis. I heard the word **crisis** in the spirit and then ministered on **a three-day event**. At my granddaughter Gabriella's (known by many as Gabrie), homegoing, as I sat on the bench listening to everyone, I said, *"Lord, what do I do? What can Gabrie, my granddaughter, speak through me to [those attending the service] that can change their lives forever?"* He told me, *"Address where they are right now."* So, I addressed where they were then and where they may be again. Likewise, I am addressing your place right now, a place of crisis.

Some of you are going through a serious crisis point in your life. Remember from an earlier chapter that the definition discussed pertained to the crisis being a problem. It was described as not just a problem, not just a happening. It's something more severe. It is something that is a terrible situation for you. The Lord told me to tell those who are in a crisis in their life right now that things are not going well. You have prayed, cried, and called your prayer partners, who are there to support and uplift you in prayer during this difficult time, but things have not changed. That's the way it is with a crisis. We can command the enemy to move; that crisis will sit right there because it tells you what you must go through. You're going to have to walk your way through this one. It is not going to roll over when you say rollover.

We're taught to speak the word, the Word of God. I'm Word conscious. On behalf of my granddaughter, we prayed around the clock for that baby. Until the Lord said, *"Hold up."* The Lord said, *"Have you asked me what My Will is?" "I've been praying your word, which is your will."* He said, *"Have you asked me for My Will?"* After that, I had to go to her mother and say, *"Charlotte, the Lord said, if we have asked Him His Will."* Well, I thought the Will was that He wanted her to live, but then I got to thinking. Hold up a second; for her to live meant that she would live in the condition that she was in. God's Will, in this context, refers to His plan and purpose for our lives, which may not always align with our desires.

Who would that benefit her or our selfishness? So, honestly, I had to inquire of the Lord. *"Lord, what are you saying? Please help me to understand because that's my grandbaby. I want her to be here for a long time. Tell me. I don't want to hold her if you say let her go. If you don't get me to let go, I'm not letting go. So, what are you saying to me?"* He then said to me, *"She talked to me on her own."* I'm thinking, *"Oh, Lord."* The whole dynamics change then. Because see, if she spoke to Him on her own, He'd consider what she said. He hears what we're saying. This now explains what she said. She, Gabrie, said, *"You know what?"* You'll understand this in a minute because she got it when I ministered on **CRISIS** and the *Three-Day Happening*, an event where God moved in a dead situation.

***

I remember hearing her playing over and over in her room, those two messages. The **CRISIS** message was found in Psalms 110, verses one and two. It talks about *sitting at my right hand until I make your enemies your footstool.* Then God said:

> *While you're going through all of the calamity, while you're going through all the pain and pressure of the sitting waiting for Me to deal with it, I don't want you to have pity parties. I want you to square your shoulders back. I want you to get up and reign.*

We can't help but to ask ourselves, *"How can I reign when I'm going through such suffering?"* Christ in you, the hope of glory. That's how you reign. What did I say? Christ in you, the hope of glory. That's how you reign.

In other words, when you're going through your tough spots, you don't act like you're going through a tough spot. When you're going through your death-like situations. You're not having pity parties. You're not crying, *"Oh, poor me."* No. You look like your Redeemer lives. You act like your Redeemer live. Did you hear what I'm saying? You square your shoulders back and say: *Come, Lord Jesus, no matter what happens, I win. I've read the end of the book. I don't lose.*

Have you read to the end of the book? If not, you need to go and visit Revelations and find out you win. You don't lose. My grandbaby played those messages repeatedly until something broke inside her; she got that, and then she said, *"Big mommy."* She said, *"I'm tired."* She said, *"I'm gonna fight now."* I said, *"Baby, stand."*

***

The Lord then gave me another word, and it dealt with Jesus when He was crucified, and they put him in the tomb; He had told everybody in three days, disciples, you walk with me. You think you know me. I'm telling you, that in three days, I won't be in there. In three days, you're going to come looking for me? Maybe some of you don't believe anything I say. Yet, I tell you what you see is not going to always be what you saw. Gabriella's leaving here took so many by surprise. They, and we, weren't expecting her to go.

They weren't expecting Jesus to be removed from that tomb. He left that place. So, you come looking for Gabriella, and Gabrie's gone because she had somewhere to go. Some might say, well, she died. However, I say, *"Death didn't hold her."* It can't keep her because she's with the Lord. She held onto Jesus. She then exited that place of containment, that tomb. For three days, death couldn't hold Jesus anymore on the third day.

On the third day, you and I have a third day coming in your life as well. On the third day, that thing will break open. On the third day, you look for God to do something. On the third day, come out of that dead place. My baby heard that message and said, *"Big mommy, on the third day."* It was on a Sunday evening when they called us to the hospital. Know this that God, make no mistakes There was Sunday evening, Monday evening, Tuesday evening, and Wednesday evening. On the third day, there was a happening. Some said, *"Well, did something happen before on the second day showed up?*' That is true, something did happen on the second day first but guess what? She came back alive.

However, on the third day, it was a wrap. It was a wrap. On the third day, she came out of that dead place that was holding her, meaning the sickness and disease. My granddaughter went from death to life, and we had a chance to witness her transition. Some of you are going through something today, or tomorrow, and the enemy is holding you or trying to. It may seem as though you can't break for yourself; the Lord said to tell you to look for your third day. Look for your third day. Remember what He has told you already. Remember what you have read already. Look unto Him, who is your faith's author and finisher. He is.

Look unto Jesus. Did you hear what I'm telling you? Say to yourself today: *I got a third day coming.* I don't know about you, but the woman of God said *a third day.* The Bible says a day is like a 1000 years, and 1000 years is like a day to the Lord. I'm not the author of time, but God is, and when God says, "*The gig is up.*" When God says, "*Your Kairos time is here,*" your third day. You shall rise from all of this despair. You shall rise from all of this pain and suffering.

You will be able to say to the enemy of your soul: You can't hold me anymore. Because when God says: *Come out, Wilma, come out. Sean, when God says, come out. Susan, when God says, come out.* You must choose to believe by faith that anything and everything that is in your way, it's got to move. They used to sing an old song; *It's Got to Move.* It's got to move. It's not going to hold you no longer. Gabrie's, my granddaughter, is gone. Her crisis is not holding her—no more. Your crisis may not be the same as her crisis, but the word of the Lord is the same for her and you. On the third day, the crisis, your and my intense situation has got to move. Say to yourself:

> *In Jesus' name, I refuse to be held by anything that's not supposed to have me. I refuse. I refuse with everything within my being; I refuse, and that is the will of God.*

Look for your third day. Look with expectancy. People might not believe you when you tell them that you're looking for your third day and that your crisis has got to move. However, it doesn't matter because when they come looking for you in that dead situation. Guess what? They won't see that situation, that crisis, anymore because you're going to be a different person and on the other side of it. God says:

> *In three days, on your third day of experience, know that I will move on your behalf.*

Say the Lord thy God.

5 RESOURCES

According as his divine power hath given unto us all things that pertain unto life and godliness, through the knowledge of him that hath called us to glory and virtue:
2 Peter 1:3

As you go through your crisis, do not forget that God is not slack in His promises (2 Peter 3:9). He is also not a man that He should lie, neither the son of man, that he should repent (Numbers 23:19; 1 Samuel 15:29). Knowing this, choose to grab hold of God's promises and the weapons that He has provided us to use during our crisis, but also when we aren't facing difficulties.

Here are some common scriptures that highlight His promises and/or the weapons that He made available to all saints of God:

Faith

Matthew 17:20 - And Jesus said unto them, Because of your unbelief:

for verily I say unto you, If ye have faith as a grain of mustard seed, ye shall say unto this mountain, Remove hence to yonder place; and it shall remove; and nothing shall be impossible unto you.

Hebrews 11:6 - But without faith it is impossible to please him: for he, that cometh to God must believe that he is, and that he is a rewarder of them that diligently seek him.

Power and Authority

2 Samuel 22:33 - God is my strength and power: and he maketh my way perfect.

Psalm 62:11 - God hath spoken once; twice have I heard this; that power belongeth unto God.

Luke 9:1-2 - ^{1}Then he called his twelve disciples together, and gave them power and authority over all devils, and to cure diseases. ^{2}And he sent them to preach the kingdom of God, and to heal the sick.

Ephesians 6:10 - Finally, my brethren, be strong in the Lord, and in the power of his might.

2 Timothy 1:7 - For God hath not given us the spirit of fear; but of power, and of love, and of a sound mind.

The Name of Jesus

Philippians 2:9-10 - ^{9}Wherefore God also hath highly exalted him, and given him a name which is above every name: ^{10}That at the name of Jesus every knee should bow, of things in heaven, and things in earth, and things under the earth;

1 Peter 3:22 - Who is gone into heaven, and is on the right hand of God; angels and authorities and powers being made subject unto him.

The Blood of Jesus

Exodus 12:23 - For the Lord will pass through to smite the Egyptians; and when he seeth the blood upon the lintel, and on the two side posts, the Lord will pass over the door, and will not suffer the destroyer to come in unto your houses to smite you.

Matthew 26:28 - For this is my blood of the new testament, which is shed for many for the remission of sins.

Revelation 12:11 - And they overcame him by the blood of the Lamb, and by the word of their testimony; and they loved not their lives unto the death.

The Word of God

Psalm 107:19-21- [19] Then they cry unto the Lord in their trouble, and he saveth them out of their distresses. [20] He sent his word, and healed them, and delivered them from their destructions.

Isaiah 55:11 - So shall my word be that goeth forth out of my mouth: it shall not return unto me void, but it shall accomplish that which I please, and it shall prosper in the thing whereto I sent it.

2 Timothy 3:16 - All scripture is given by inspiration of God, and is profitable for doctrine, for reproof, for correction, for instruction in righteousness:

Hebrews 4:12 - For the word of God is quick, and powerful, and sharper than any two-edged sword, piercing even to the dividing asunder of soul and spirit, and of the joints and marrow, and is a discerner of the thoughts and intents of the heart.

Praise

Psalm 9:1-2 – [1]I will praise thee, O Lord, with my whole heart; I will shew forth all thy marvellous works. [2]I will be glad and rejoice in thee: I will sing praise to thy name, O thou most High.

Psalm 28:7 - The Lord is my strength and my shield; my heart trusted in him, and I am helped: therefore, my heart greatly rejoiceth; and with my song will I praise him.

Psalm 55:22 - Cast thy burden upon the Lord, and he shall sustain thee: he shall never suffer the righteous to be moved.

1 Thessalonians 5:18 - In every thing give thanks: for this is the will of God in Christ Jesus concerning you.

Hebrews 13:15 - By him therefore let us offer the sacrifice of praise to God continually, that is, the fruit of our lips giving thanks to his name.

Armor of God

Ephesians 6:9-11 - [9]And, ye masters, do the same things unto them, forbearing threatening: knowing that your Master also is in heaven; neither is there respect of persons with him. [10]Finally, my brethren, be strong in the Lord, and in the power of his might. [11]Put on the whole armour of God, that ye may be able to stand against the wiles of the devil.

Prayer

Romans 8:26 - Likewise the Spirit also helpeth our infirmities: for we know not what we should pray for as we ought: but the Spirit itself maketh intercession for us with groanings which cannot be uttered.

Philippians 4:6-7 - ⁶ Be careful for nothing; but in every thing by prayer and supplication with thanksgiving let your requests be made known unto God. ⁷ And the peace of God, which passeth all understanding, shall keep your hearts and minds through Christ Jesus.

1 John 5:14-15 - ¹⁴ And this is the confidence that we have in him, that, if we ask any thing according to his will, he heareth us: ¹⁵ And if we know that he hear us, whatsoever we ask, we know that we have the petitions that we desired of him.

Prayer & Confession: Binding and Loosing

Matthew 16:19 - And I will give unto thee the keys of the kingdom of heaven: and whatsoever thou shalt bind on earth shall be bound in heaven: and whatsoever thou shalt loose on earth shall be loosed in heaven.

Matthew 18:18 - Verily I say unto you, Whatsoever ye shall bind on earth shall be bound in heaven: and whatsoever ye shall loose on earth shall be loosed in heaven.

Prayer & Confession: Declaring and Decreeing

Job 22:28 - Thou shalt also decree a thing, and it shall be established unto thee: and the light shall shine upon thy ways.

Romans 4:17 - (As it is written, I have made thee a father of many nations,) before him whom he believed, even God, who quickeneth the dead, and calleth those things which be not as though they were.

To Be Declared

Isaiah 54:17 - No weapon that is formed against thee shall prosper; and every tongue that shall rise against thee in judgment thou shalt condemn. This is the heritage of the servants of the Lord, and their righteousness is of me, saith the Lord.

Psalm 23:1 - The Lord is my shepherd; I shall not want.

Psalm 24:1 - The earth is the Lord's, and the fulness thereof; the world, and they that dwell therein.

Psalm 118:17 - I shall not die, but live, and declare the works of the Lord.

Philippians 4:13 - I can do all things through Christ which strengtheneth me.

Hebrews 10:38 - Now the just shall live by faith:

Add your own favorite scriptures to stand on during your crisis:

_____

_____

_____

In addition to God's written Word serving as an encouragement and a weapon, music can serve as a support and a reminder of what has spoken. The following is a list of suggested song themes that may be helpful when researching songs to encourage yourself with.

Suggested Song Themes
Look for songs that promote or talk about...

- "The Just" living by faith
- Having God's perfect peace
- The Lord being the Lord of our breakthrough
- Having the victory
- Speaking the Word of God
- Praising God in every circumstances

AFTERWORD

This book was about what you and I do when we are in a time of crisis. All that I know is that crises come into our lives. No one is exempt. No person – no race, no gender, no age, no profession, and no economic position – is exempt. We will all experience crises at some time in life. It then becomes vital that we learn how to navigate crises and be encouraged to look to God to help us be victorious through it and obtain the promise of the eradication of it.

***

Knowing that just because we have a crisis does not mean that we have to bow down and buckle under the crisis. For many of us, no one ever told us we could stand firm during the crisis. In fact, no one ever told us this is what God expects from us. God wants to take us to a place, but He can't take us there if we're unwilling to see Him or expect Him to take us there. Additionally, on top of that, let Him take us there. Let Him take us to a place of reigning, ruling through adversity and disappointment. God knows we've had it. This teaching was born out of crisis. It was birthed through seasons of deep, strong, hard places of crisis. And God had to say: *You know what? I am your Comforter, but I need to tell you how I will comfort you.*

Many people think God solely comforts them by wrapping His arms around them. In this case, He comforts us by showing us the strength of who He is in us. By this, He says, what?

> *Get up. Rise up. Square your shoulders back. Don't be afraid to stare at the situation in the face because he [the enemy] can look at you and hates you. However, he [the enemy of your and my soul] can't have us.*

So, come on and let's go, and reign and rule in our crisis **until** God makes our crisis situations our footstool.

ABOUT THE AUTHOR

Wilma C. Foster is the Senior Pastor of Breakthrough Ministries, Inc. She is also the CEO/Founder of the Daughters of Deborah Ministries, Inc., a non-profit organization dedicated to empowering women in the community, and Project Youth Wellness, a youth-focused initiative that promotes physical, mental, and spiritual health.

Called to the pastorate in her early thirties, Pastor Foster operates under an apostolic-prophetic anointing. She is called to "hurting" people and has worked to help them make it through tough times by personally demonstrating God's great love for them, teaching them how to navigate difficulties, and inspiring them to embrace God's promises.

Pastor Wilma C. Foster is married to Apostle Henry A. Foster. She is the mother of four children and the grandmother of more than ten grandchildren. She also has many spiritual sons, daughters, and grandchildren.

Reaching, teaching, and inspiring people of ages to see their greatness and fulfil their given life's purpose.

CRISIS

No matter what the crisis is, you can rule in the midst.

Wilma Foster

Our books are available at special quantity discounts for bulk purchases for sales promotions, fundraising, or educational use.

To order bulk copies for giveaways, distribution to church members or groups, sales promotions, or education, contact:

Daughters of Deborah Ministries, Inc.
Wichita, Kansas 67206
Phone: (316) 202-8988
Email: DoDMinistriesInc@gmail.com

* 9 7 8 1 9 3 0 1 8 3 1 2 4 *